MW00936093

Stock

Trading

The Definitive Beginner's
Guide - Make Money Trading The
Stock Market Like A Pro

by Adam Rirchards

Table of Contents

Introduction

"I always knew I was going to be rich. I don't think I ever doubted it for a minute."

- Warren Buffett

The question is, do you? Let's start with that thought first, because it's a given that you really 'are' what you think. As for the means to getting there, don't worry. We've got you covered. That's why this book has been designed especially for you – the newbie looking to make it big in the world of stock trading.

How stock trading works is simple, really. They are traded on exchanges, which are really places where buyers and sellers meet and decide on a price. You've probably seen innumerable instances of trading floors in the movies, where people are yelling with their arms in the air. Well okay, that's one way in which stocks are traded. They can also be traded electronically, through a network of computers.

It's important that you learn the pivotal difference between stock trading and stock 'investing' before we are to continue on an in-depth analysis of the former along the course of this book. Stock investing is the process of gradually building your wealth over time through the buying and holding of stock scripts, mutual funds and other investment tools. On the other hand, trading involves the more frequent buying and selling of stocks and commodities with a view to generating quick returns.

The profits that are accrued in trading are generated through buying at a low price and selling at a higher price in a short period of time. They don't wait out the low price levels as do trading investors, but rather close at a predetermined price level. Let's begin then, and delve into the world of stock trading to see how we can leverage ourselves to become skilled stock traders before we can get down on that 'trading' floor and rock it!

Chapter 1:

Stock Market Essentials

Of course, you're dying to know how the 'system' works in order to forge a way into the intricate maze that is called the stock market that will lead to those awesome profits and make you richer beyond that which you could imagine. But first let's take a look at the essentials that surround stocks and the stock market, in order to have a strong base for which we can lay our stock trading skills.

So let's begin, then, by asking ourselves the question, 'What are stocks?' That's a highly relevant question, considering we will be going into them in deeper detail over the course of this book. In a nutshell, a stock is a 'share in the ownership of a company'. When you acquire more stocks your share in the ownership of the company increases subsequently, of course. You might use different words like 'shares', equities' and 'stocks' but they really all mean the same thing.

When you hold a company's 'stock' it really means that you are an 'owner' of the said company, no matter how small the percentage of stock that you might be holding. This means that you have an actual 'claim' to the profits of that company and even the voting rights that can play a crucial role in determining its future. A stock used to be represented by a 'stock certificate', which as the name suggests was a fancy piece of paper but in today's day and age everything is done electronically so you don't really need that piece of paper at all.

So why does a company issue stock at all? Well of course it is because it needs to raise money. That's where stock traders like you step in. Of course, you have an ulterior motive yourself. You want to make money through the process of trading those stocks. That doesn't really affect the company in question. The ownership simply passes on to another person; you make your profit and everyone ion the equation seems to be happy.

Now the very basic premise behind a stock market is that it exists to facilitate the buying and selling of stocks out there, which means that your risk of investing is minimized. We need to first understand the difference between the two 'market's involved, the primary market and the secondary market. The primary market is where the securities are created (via an IPO) and the secondary market is a place where traders 'trade' these securities freely without the involvement of the issuing companies.

Let us look at some of the stock markets that are primordial in the selling of those 'stocks'.

The New York Stock Exchange (NYSE)

It is the most renowned stock exchange in the world. It is the market of choice for the largest and most prestigious companies in America. The NYSE is the first kind of exchange where the trading takes place 'on the floor'. This is also referred to as a 'listed exchange'. How things work here are like this: the orders come in from the members of the exchange (brokerage firms) and trickle down to the floor brokers who go to a specific place on the 'trading floor' where the stock is actually traded.

Here prices are determined by an 'auction method' by a person called the 'specialist' whose job is to match buyers and sellers. How the auction method works is like this: the current price is the highest amount a buyer is willing to pay and the lowest amount at which someone is willing to sell. Once the deal is made, the information is conveyed to the brokerage firm who then informs the investor that the trade has been made. Of course this is an exchange that relies heavily on human connection but nevertheless it is backed by some of the best computer technology.

Nasdaq

This is a virtual, over-the-counter type of stock market where the trading takes place via computers and through a telecommunications network of dealers. There is no central location and floor brokers as in the case of the NYSE. The Nasdaq is a serious competitor to the NYSE, with several large companies like Microsoft and Oracle being listed on it.

On the Nasdaq a 'market broker' will provide continuous bid and ask prices that fall within a prescribed percentage spread for shares for which they are designated to make a market. They might even match buyers and sellers directly but usually they maintain an inventory of shares to meet the demands of investors.

Other Exchanges

The American Stock Exchange is the third largest stock market in the U.S., with mainly small-cap stocks and derivatives trading on it. However, there are many other stock exchanges in different parts of the world that do a lot of business as well, besides the American one. The London Stock Exchange and Hong Kong Stock Exchange are prime examples of stock exchanges that do a good deal of trading business.

The thing to remember when you are going to be trading is this: that stock prices fluctuate daily because of the market forces out there. That means that it all comes down to supply and demand as far as the prices of those stocks is concerned. Thus, if there is more 'demand' for a stock then the price will go up while if there is less 'demand' and more 'supply', the price will decrease.

The most common method to purchase stocks is through a brokerage. There are two different types of brokerage. The full-service brokerages charge a lot for offering you expert advice and even for managing your account. On the other hand, discount brokerages offer a lot less as far as personal attention is concerned, but are really much cheaper. These are the online discount brokers and thanks to them, it is easy for almost everyone out there to invest in the stock market.

It's impossible to close this chapter without discussing what the 'bulls and bears' are all about. It's not half as dicey as explaining the 'birds and bees' to your teenage child, though. Let's take a look at what these terms that you will hear every now and then whilst in the process of stock trading, really mean.

Bulls

A 'bull' market is one in which everything seems to be going just great; the economy is superlative, GDP is rising and people are getting jobs. Of course it is really most easy to pick up your stocks in this kind of market because everything is really going 'up'. A person who is optimistic and feels that the stock price will only go 'up', is called a 'bull'. Of course the drawback is that a bull market cannot last forever and sometimes the stock prices get overvalued.

Bears

A bear market is just the opposite of the 'Bull' market. This is when recession has kicked in and investors are finding it hard to pick stocks. People either 'short sell' in this case to make money or wait the 'bearish' period through and then start to buy in anticipation of the stocks going up. A person, who is pessimistic and thinks the stocks are going to fall, is called a 'bear'.

Chapter 2:

15 Rules For Successful Stock Trading

Now that we've gotten a gist of what stocks and trading with them is all about, let's look at the 15 most important 'rules' that need to be strictly adhered to in order to ensure that our process of trading goes off without a glitch.

Rule No1: Do not put all your cash on the table at once.

In Vegas you don't wish to put all your money on the color 'red' before you sit back and watch that roulette wheel spin, do you? There will be opportunities that come to you all the time; perhaps even better opportunities than that which you have at the present moment. Allow room for those opportunities to happen by keeping cash on hand, always.

Rule No2: Forge a plan.

It is most sensible to allocate predetermined points at which you can cut losses or take those profits.

Rule No3: Don't wait too long to take those profits.

You have to remember this: that the market can reverse just as easily as it rose in the very first place. If you have a sizeable profit that has been sitting there awhile, it would suit you best to take it. You could use the money very well to buy that next stock you have been looking at for some time.

Rule No4: Find out the events that move markets.

You need to do some pretty solid research on which events tend to move markets. Read financial publications to gain a sense into how world events affect the market out there so that you can be prepared for the same.

Rule No5: Minimize those transaction costs.

You need to understand that there are costs involved in stock trading; things like taxes and brokerage fees and that you really do need to minimize those transaction costs if you want to make sure that you are going to make profits in the long run.

Rule No6: Understand the beta of a stock.

The beta of the stock refers to its volatility. The more volatile a stock is, the more it will tend to fall when the index goes down. This also means that it has the capacity to rise even higher than other stocks that have a lower beta than it. Therefore it would be smart to consider stocks with a higher beta in the case of stock trading, in order to maximize your profits. Make sure that you regularly check the stock's beta.

Rule No7: Make sure that you learn the value of 'patience'.

It's easy to become scared and even greedy when people all around you are doing things that you feel you need to be doing. Observe people in an attempt to learn from them but don not change your overall strategy to suit theirs. You have to remember that ultimately if you are to make a difference it will be through your own unique strategizing and thinking processes. Keep calm at all times in an attempt to strive towards trading excellence.

Rule No8: Check out the trading history of the stock.

There are charts and other sources of data out there that will tell you how well a stock has moved in recent weeks and months. You need to analyze this data carefully in order to gauge any seasonality or patterns therein that would enable you to make future predictions as far as the stock is concerned.

Rule No9: Find out those hedging techniques.

These are techniques that are designed to protect you when the market goes down. No matter how 'bullish' you are, it won't hurt to be most well prepared when it comes to the future; you never quite know when things might get 'bearish' for you. So make sure you employ those hedging techniques well.

Rule No10: Make sure that you book those losses well.

You might think that it is all about booking those profits but it is equally if not more, important to book those 'losses' as well before they spiral out of control.

Rule No11: Make sure that you use that stop loss order well.

If you don't then you will find that the market will move against you the next day. Whatever you do, make sure that you don't cancel that stop order. That might only serve to ensure that you lose even more money in the process.

Rule No12: Make sure that you follow the 'trend'.

This might just be the safest thing you could ever do.

You might be averse to buying high and selling low, but it might just be the right thing to do if everyone out there is already doing it. There's a reason behind there being a 'trend', after all; make sure that you follow it.

Rule No13: Invest in multiple sectors.

It would be most prudent to invest in multiple sectors in order to 'play it safe'. Invest in three or four sectors instead of putting all your eggs in one basket!

Rule No14: Trade wisely and book profits in a timely fashion.

You might wish to not invest all of the money you have predetermined for the purpose of trading. Make sure that you trade only half the affixed amount. As far as profits are concerned, we have discussed that it would merit you to take those profits if they have been sitting out there for long; at the same time you want those profits to grow a little; wait until the opportune moment comes to pluck those 'profits' from the 'tree of stocks'.

Rule No15: Step out of the trade in a graceful fashion.

You have to be prepared for the fact that you will not make money on all your trades. You have to know when to exit when you find that things are going wrong and that you do not change your pre-existing strategy, which might just end up mean you end up making far more losses than anticipated.

Chapter 3:

9 Mistakes Most Beginner Traders Make (And How To Avoid Them)

Now that we've taken a look at the proverbial list of 'to dos' as far as rookie traders such as yourself are concerned, let's take a look at the 9 most common 'mistakes' that are made by beginner traders in an attempt to rectify them and move along the path towards success in our stock trading endeavors.

Mistake No1: They add to losing positions'.

It's most common for rookie traders out there to add to 'losing positions' in an attempt to turn things around, but that might just be the last thing that they needed to do.

Solution: If you really need to turn things around you need to do more of what is working and less of what does not, in order to make sure you don't drive yourself deep into loss.

Mistake No2: Making those trades out of 'boredom'.

Sometimes new traders find themselves unable to even sit for a moment without making a trade, simply because they find it too 'boring' to do nothing, considering the fact that up till now they have been most active in the trading process. As a result they do a trade without doing the appropriate and most essential research behind it.

Solution: You cannot afford to be in a position where you make those trades simply because you have been habituated to so doing. It's much better to be bored and wait things out until the right moment comes to invest again, which will be sooner than you expected.

Mistake No3: They keep moving from one strategy to the next.

Of course if you kept on making money all the time through the process of your newfound trading activity, you wouldn't find yourself in a situation like this at all. If things are really going askew for you, it is certainly not prudent to keep juggling your way through various strategies.

Solution: Things might not be all that rosy at times but if you have the discipline to stick to the strategy that you have implemented; it will be well worth your while in the end. You have to give your strategy enough time to work and banish that losing streak!

Mistake No4: They don't have an exit plan.

This is the commonest mistake that most new traders make. They don't have an exit plan and just keep those losing stocks for far longer than they should have ever kept them. That just results in them ending up as 'dead stocks', something that is most clearly detrimental to your business of stock trading.

Solution: The thing you need to do whenever you buy a stock is to put in your stop loss once you get your 'fill'. This means that you will know when you are going to be getting out. That means having a proper exit plan which will entail just how much money you are prepared to lose right before buying the stock itself! Of course this exit should be based on a logical method of thinking such as determining that whenever it falls below that support area, it should no longer be held and therefore gotten rid of.

Mistake No5: They go in for impulsive trading.

While it is advisable to stay with the trends most of the time as we have discussed already in the previous chapter as far as stock trading is concerned, it might not really be the best thing to do, to end up trading rather impulsively simply because there is a trend in the market out there that you need to 'follow'. Oftentimes these trends are not backed by good solid research.

Solution: No matter which way the trends point, you have to make sure that you do the requisite market research on your very own before you actually go towards following that trend in an attempt to garner more profits.

Mistake No6: They lack the much-needed discipline that is needed for swing trading.

What they do is more often than not wait too long

or too less before they make their entry or exit. This only results in getting that 'market timing' wrong and not ending up doing as well as they might have expected.

Solution: You need to have the discipline to wait for just the perfect market conditions and make trades that are high in probability in order to avoid those huge losses that you might if you push those limits too much.

Mistake No7: They don't have a strategy at all.

A few points earlier we just discussed how it is most wise to not have too many strategies where it comes to the process of that stock trading business of yours, but the worst possible thing you could do is to not have a strategy at all in the first place.

Solution: You need the patience to work on a strategy that seems plausible enough to work in an environment that is indeed most competitive out there. Otherwise you will simply find yourself short of having any sense of direction at all and lose your way in the dark.

Mistake No8: They overestimate how much they should invest at any given time.

They take position sizes that are too large for their portfolio. What compounds the problem is when they don't use stop losses in the trades that go against them.

Solution: You need to only take on that which you are capable of taking on. That way you will always find yourself in a most realistic situation, one that has stop losses as well in order to ensure that when things do go wrong, they do not go terribly askew.

Mistake No9: They listen too much to those 'pundits' out there.

There are so many people out there advising you on what to do when it comes to maximizing profits in stock trading, but that might just not be the perfect advice for you, as you might find out rather harshly later on.

Solution: Stick to your own strategy and zone out the world outside. The 'pundits' are in all probability not actively trading themselves; besides, when things go wrong it's really 'you' that will have to find a way out of the mess, not them.

Chapter 4:

The Benefits And Risks Of Stop-Loss And Stop-Limit Orders

When traders are looking to minimize their losses, there are two kinds of 'orders' that will help them set things 'in order' once again. These are the 'stop-loss' and 'stop-limit' orders. Let us take a look at each of them, first, in an attempt to understand exactly what they mean.

Stop-Loss Orders

There are two types of stop-loss orders. Let us take a look at each of them.

Sell-stop orders.

These are the ones that protect long positions that trigger a 'market sell' order if the price happens to fall below a certain level. The philosophy behind this is that if the price of the stock has fallen thus far, it might even fall much further, and so by selling at this price the loss can be effectively capped.

#*Buy-stop orders.*

These are the ones that are used to protect the 'short positions'. In concept they are the same as sell-stop orders. Thus a buy-stop order will be above the current price and will be triggered if the price rises above that level.

Stop-Limit Orders

These are similar to the stop-loss orders discussed above, but the difference lies in the limit on the price at which they are executed. There are two prices that are specified in a stop-limit order, the 'stop price' that will convert the price into a sell order, and the 'limit price'. The sell order thus becomes a limit order that will execute at the limit price or better. These are used because sometimes when the stock price falls below the limit, the shareholder can decide whether he or she does indeed want to sell or rather wait for the price to rise back to the limit price.

Now that we have seen the differences between stop-loss orders and stop-limit orders, let us find out the benefits and the risks that are associated with both of them, with a view to understanding just how and when we need to implement them in that stock trading process of ours.

The Benefits And Risks Of Stop-Loss Orders

Benefits

\# They can be used to limit losses and guarantee profits by ensuring that the stock is sold before it falls below the purchasing price.

\# Stop-loss orders take the emotion out of the process of buying and selling. It helps you develop pre-determined entry and exit criteria and thus helps you be most 'neutral' when it comes to the buying and selling process, making sure that your emotions do not get in the way.

\# You can consider them as an extra cost that you absorb to allow for the lack of the time that you need to analyze.

Risks

\# The exit prices are based solely on falling prices, which might not be all that useful indicators of something being wrong. To sell merely because the price is falling might not be the opportune thing to do because the same risk of price fluctuation' will be associated with other shares in the market. It might be all the more relevant to set up a stop loss in regards to a particular 'sector' or market.

A stop-loss places too much importance on capital return rather than income return. The thing to realize here is that income return is just as important as capital return.

It only serves to highlight your losses. Imagine the scenario where you might buy a share that was more than 20 percent off on its market 'high'. If you would 'buy' at that price, then why wouldn't you hold on to that very price which is really nothing but that 'stop-loss' price at which you are now looking to sell?

You might sell lower than the stop order itself. When a stop order is triggered it will initiate the process of selling the stock, which might really end up being sold

at lesser than the price the stop order is set at because it is not instantaneous.

The Benefits And Risks Of Stop-Limit Orders

Benefits

They allow the investor to control the price at which a particular order is executed. What's more, the stop price and limit price do not have to be the same.

They are 'price-oriented'. When you use a stop-limit order, you wait until the price of the stock reaches a certain point and then explain the price that you will take from that point onwards. That helps you hone in on those invaluable profits. When you are in the process of selling, the stop portion of the order will trigger a sale if your stock hits a price that suggests that you will lose money. The 'limit' portion of your order will protect you from an extremely low price coming in once that order is active.

Risks

\# The trade may not be executed. This might not work out all that well for the potential investor, who might find themselves incurring substantial losses because the limit price might not get filled before the market price drops below that amount.

\# This involves a higher commission from stockbrokers and is not even executed if the limit price is not reached. What's worse, it might be triggered by short-term market fluctuations, which is something you really do not want at all.

When you ultimately set off in choosing which of the above orders is better for you to use, it's really all about considering which risks you are better suited to take on. Of course you must do some rather stellar research into the stock; if it is volatile then you might consider using a stop-limit order in lieu of its price guarantee. A stop-loss order on the other hand, would be good in the case there is some bad news about a company, which means that its price might not rise substantially for years to come.

In a nutshell, stop-loss orders guarantee execution while stop-limit orders, price. Make sure to choose the one that works best for you!

Chapter 5:

The Basics Of Fundamental

Analysis

Fundamental analysis in its most basic essence is the process of determining the value of a security by focusing on the underlying factors that affect the actual business of the company and its future prospects. Therefore it strives to answer the most basic questions that everyone needs to ask of the company they are investing in; things like 'Is the company's revenue growing?' and 'Is it able to repay its debts?' In a nutshell, fundamental analysis strives to answer the question as to whether the stock of a company is really a good investment, after all.

To understand more about fundamental analysis, it is essential to have an understanding as to what the 'fundamentals' involved really are. The fundamental factors here are grouped into two categories, which are the following.

#Quantitative

These are capable of being measured or expressed in numerical terms. In this context the quantitative fundamentals refer to the measurable characteristics of the business, which are to be found in those financial statements.

#Qualitative

These are related to the quality or character of something, as opposed to its size or quantity. These are factors that are really not all that tangible when it comes to gauging the effectiveness of a company's stock, but nonetheless quite revelatory. These include things like the quality of the board members of a company and its patents or perhaps even technology that is proprietary.

So how do we go about conducting a thorough fundamental analysis so that we can come to a decision as to whether we should be investing in a particular company's stocks or not? Let's take a look at the process of fundamental analysis in an attempt to understand just that!

How To Perform Fundamental Analysis

Before we start conducting that fundamental analysis it is important to get an idea of the documents that will be needed in order to conduct the same. Here's a look at the same.

#Quarterly financial report

This will give you an idea of how a company's just-completed quarter went. The key financial measures like revenue, expenses and profits are integral in determining the current 'health' of a business.

The Annual Financial Report

This is probably the most important document that you will need to conduct that fundamental analysis. This covers all the developments of the company and financial statements for the entire year.

Income Statement

This one's really important. It shows you all the 'money' that is coming into the company as well as the actual 'profit' it makes after cutting its costs.

Balance Sheet

This will give you an idea of what the company owns, and what it 'owes', as well.

The cash flow statement

While the income statement and balance sheet might be most important in deducing the overall health of a company in the process of determining whether one should invest in it or not, the cash flow system is nonetheless crucial because it gives a real tangible image of the 'cash' that is coming into the company.

Performing Fundamental Analysis

Compare the current year's annual report with last year's.

You want to know if the company has exceeded last year's figures. That's a good thing. If not, you want to find out the flaws in management that might have led to the decrease and if you should even be investing in the company after all.

Compare cash flow with net income

You want to make sure that the company is bringing in around the same amount of 'cash' as the profit that is reported.

Check those operating and gross margins

This helps you see the amount of profit a company generates in relation to its revenue.

Monitor that 'executive pay'

In an annual report you will find something called a 'proxy statement'. This will give you an idea of what the top executives in the company are earning. If the figures are substantially higher than they should be, you might wish to reconsider investing because that shows that it really might be all about 'themselves' for the upper echelons of management and not about the investor.

Look for potential 'conflicts of interest'

You might wish to scout for things in the proxy statement that might indicate that one of the directors has business dealings with the company. That's not an ideal situation and you might even consider withholding your vote for them.

Checklist To Identify Profitable Stocks Using Fundamental Analysis

#Look at the 'earnings per share' in that fundamental analysis.

This will help you indicate the growth rate and profitability of the company. This is found by taking the number of common stock shares that are outstanding and dividing them into the company's profits after taxes.

#Use 'stock chart analysis'

This way, you can understand the price pattern of the stock. This will help you accurately predict if the price will go up or down.

#Only compare stocks in the same industry against one another

That is the only way that you will ensure that the comparison is accurate.

#Look at the earnings history for at least the last three years

Even a company that is public for a short period of time will have this information from the time before the IPO was launched, when it was private.

#Look at the sales of the company for at least the last six quarters

It should be 'growing', at least over the course of the last four quarters.

#The 'return on equity' percentage should be evaluated

It should be at least twenty percent or more.

#Look for stocks in companies that offer unique products

This only means greater demand for the product and hence increased profitability for the company.

Chapter 6:

Technical Analysis Simplified

So, what is 'technical analysis', you might ask? Well, it is all about studying the stock price graphs. In the previous chapter we discussed what fundamental analysis is all about. This is most different from fundamental analysis in the fact that it does not hinge on the premise that you can deduce the viability of a stock through things like quarterly results and balance sheets. If they were so important then the prices of stocks would really change far more often than say 4 or 5 times a year; the very reason that they change almost every day is an indicator that there must be afar advanced methodology that is required to understand the viability of a stock.

In essence fundamental analysis is a methodology for forecasting the direction of prices through the study of past market data, primarily price and volume.

How To Perform Efficient Technical Analysis

If one wishes to do an efficient technical analysis in order to determine if a company's stock is indeed viable or not, then one must use 'indicators' that can be used as a measure to gain unique insight into the supply and demand of securities. These indicators confirm price movement and the probability that the said move will continue in the future.

Therefore these indicators can help you to a great

extent in the buying and selling process. Let us take a look, then, at three of the most important indicators that can be used most effectively for that technical analysis of ours.

MACD

On a trading chart, the 'Moving Average Convergence-Divergence Indicator' (MACD) was initially designed to use exponential moving averages of 26 and 12 days, although you can use any moving average that suits your fancy. A complete MACD indicator includes an indicator line and a trigger (which is a moving average of the indicator, superimposed on top of the indicator).

With a MACD chart you will see three numbers that are used for its settings.

The first is the number of periods that is used to calculate the faster moving average.

The second is used to calculate the slower moving average.

\# The third is the number of bars that is used to calculate the moving average of the difference between the faster and slower moving averages

The faster moving average will be quicker to react to price movement than the slower one. So when a new trend occurs the fast line will react and soon cross the slower one. This 'crossover' indicates the emergence of the new trend itself.

RSI

This is one of the most popular technical indicators and is calculated based on the speed and direction of a stock's price movement. This is an excellent way to measure the internal strength of a stock (based on its past). The RSI is calculated using a process that involves two steps. Firstly, the average gains and losses are identified for a specific time period. Most commonly a period of 14 days is used for the computation of that RSI.

Now suppose the stock goes up by ten days and falls

by four days within that stipulated period of time. Then, the absolute gains (which are the stock's closing price on that day minus the closing price on the previous day) are added up and divided by 14 in order to get the 'average gains'. In a similar way the 'average losses' are also deduced. The ratio between these values is known as the "Relative Strength'. This will vary between 0 and 100 and is an excellent indicator of the strength of a stock where it comes to the pivotal decision of whether one must invest in it or not.

Stochastic

The Stochastic is an oscillator that measures overbought and oversold conditions in the market. It is scored from 0 to 100. When the Stochastic lines are above 80 then it means that the market is overbought. On the other hand, when the Stochastic lines are below 20, then it means that it is oversold. As a rule you must remember that you buy when the market is oversold and sell when the market is overbought.

48

Criteria To Keep In Mind When Identifying Entry And Exit Points

It really comes all down to that crucial sense of timing as far as making an entry or exit in the market is concerned.

Entry Point Criteria

You need to make sure that you enter based on the trend that is dominant in the market. That will ensure that you have a low-risk entry and high potential for profit.

At the same time you need to ensure that you invest your capital in a 'layered' manner which means that you do not use all of it at once but instead continue to add to it in a most structure manner so that the high risk that is associated with the investment is minimized.

There will be times when the risk/reward ratio will

be so positive that you will not have to invest in a layered manner but rather put 'all your eggs in one basket', after all. In these cases the exact price where the position is opened is really not all that important, after all.

Exit Point Criteria

\# Make sure that you create that exit strategy before you even get in the trade. That will ensure that your emotions do not get in the way and that the exit strategy is based on the clinical 'technical analysis data' that you have garnered.

\# Use a simple risk/ reward ratio to determine your exit along with a sizeable profit, something like a 1: 2 ratio.

Of course there's no hard rule when it comes to setting those entry and exit points in the market out there. To a large degree it depends on the amount of risk that you as an individual are prepared to take. So along with those technical analysis tools, you might wish to give a little leeway to that 'gut instinct' of yours, as well!

Chapter 7:

Trading Platforms Or Online Brokers

This is the proverbial question that is asked by one and all that enter the exciting new realm of stock trading. Of course both have their pros and cons and the purpose of this chapter is to help you make that crucial decision a whole lot easier. Let's begin then by taking a closer look at the process of online trading and how it scores those brownie points over the traditional system of trading with a broker.

In the process of online trading, brokers buy and sell stocks through an exchange and charge a commission to do the same. A broker is a person who is licensed to sell stocks through an exchange. So what you really doing in the process of buying and selling stocks online, is using an online broker that takes the place of a 'human' broker in the erstwhile traditional process of broking. So what are the advantages of online trading as compared to the traditional system?

Let's take a look and find out with a view to finding a system that works best for us.

Cost

This is by far one of the biggest benefits that online broking has to offer. Traditional brokers usually charge a brokerage fee that is quite stiff as well as a percentage of the profits that you earn, on account of the expertise they bring to your business. On the other hand online brokerage firms charge flat, inexpensive rates for each transaction.

Convenience

You can buy or sell the shares at any given point in time, according to your convenience. You can make changes in that online trading process any time you want and view your account and see how your investments are doing. This sort of convenience is not afforded by the traditional method of broking. The traditional method of broking operates within fixed hours whereas in the online system you can really operate that account of yours 24/7.

Information

You are really privy to a vast wealth of information when you opt in for those online trading services. You can even customize your account page in order to display the trends and stocks that they might be interested in. Of course in today's competitive world you will find that the traditional brokers too have gotten into this process of supplying this valuable information, but be warned that it comes at a cost that is significantly higher than that compared with what is involved in opting for the relatively inexpensive online trading system.

Of course there are some people out there who might like the 'human touch' when it comes to getting valuable information and if you are one of them you might wish to settle for the traditional system of broking itself. At the end of the day you really need to be comfortable with whatever system you choose to take that process of stock broking forward.

Criteria In Selecting A Stellar Online Trading Platform

#You want to select one that is experienced and reliable

All you need to do is a little bit of research into finding out exactly how many years the company has been around and its track record. You don't want a company that is relatively new; always go in for the ones with a solid track record and impeccable credentials.

#Good customer service

Opting for an online broking service means that you have a greater degree of control in the manner you manage those stocks. But that doesn't mean that you will have to find it difficult to get help when the time comes; and there will be plenty of times, mind you. Make sure you select an online broking firm with an unparalleled level of customer service in an attempt to ensure the same.

#Make sure that the service provides you rapid account updates

You need to have those updates to your account by the beginning of each business day at least, after the completion of your order. Some services will offer you streaming information as well for information on those quotes, but they usually carry a high premium and are prone to transmission delays.

#Make sure that there is instant communication

of the execution of those orders

You need to be instantly alerted whenever that order of yours is executed. You cannot sit around waiting for a statement to be delivered in the mail; if anything goes wrong, the delay might cause you a lot of money to rectify the same.

#Make sure that the brokers offer low margin rates

Most brokers out there offer margin rates that allow you to borrow against the equity in your account to buy more stocks. Make sure that those rates are low, not higher than seven percent.

Conclusion

'Rule 1: Never lose money

Rule 2: Never forget Rule 1'

- Warren Buffett

How true! But also very difficult when it comes down to the actual business of trading stocks. There will be times when you might find yourself tearing out your hair because you are losing more money than you ever thought you would but the key to finding salvation in the above italicized quote by the legendary Warren Buffet himself is to have persistence.

Over the course of this book you have seen all the possible ways you can take control over the reins of stock trading and navigate your way towards those profits. But then this book never told you it was going to be easy.

The stock market might be a very challenging place to be in but once you have entered and spent some time in it whilst at the same time incorporating the tenets that this book has proposed, you will understand the finer nuances on a greater level and work your way towards even greater profitability in the time to come.

So what are you waiting for? It's about time you got started in the world of stock trading and worked your way towards minting those 'pots of money' you've always dreamed of!

I will be more than happy to learn how this book has helped you in some way. If you feel you have learned something or you think it offered you some value, please take a moment to leave an honest review on Amazon. It would help many future readers who will be forever grateful to you. As I will!

To Your Success,
Adam Richards

DISCLAIMER AND/OR LEGAL NOTICES:

CPSIA information can be obtained at www.ICGtesting.com
Printed in the USA
LVOW08s0005160915

454272LV00022B/516/P